Edna Mae Burnam's PIANO COURSE

with

Close-Phased Grading

PHASE 2
Five – Finger Fluency

THE WILLIS MUSIC COMPANY

© 1959, Revised © 1967 The Willis Music Company, Florence, KY, US, All Rights Reserved

ISBN: 978-0-7119-5683-4

For all works contained herein:
Unauthorized copying, arranging, adapting, recording, internet posting, public performance,
or other distribution of the music in this publication is an infringement of copyright.
Infringers are liable under the law.

Visit Hal Leonard Online at
www.halleonard.com

World headquarters, contact:
Hal Leonard
7777 West Bluemound Road
Milwaukee, WI 53213
Email: info@halleonard.com

In Europe, contact:
Hal Leonard Europe Limited
1 Red Place
London, W1K 6PL
Email: info@halleonardeurope.com

In Australia, contact:
Hal Leonard Australia Pty. Ltd.
4 Lentara Court
Cheltenham, Victoria, 3192 Australia
Email: info@halleonard.com.au

FOREWORD

MINISTEPS TO MUSIC, Phase II, develops the pattern of tuition established in the previous book. Again the aim is to encourage keyboard facility and promote a sensitive musicality at an inflexibly defined rate of progress — CLOSE-PHASED GRADING. Professional comment on CLOSE-PHASED GRADING has centred favourably on the greater scope for application of acquired techniques — practical and theoretical — that it affords the young musician. This fluency creates a sense of accomplishment which invariably stimulates the pupil to greater effort.

EDNA MAE BURNAM

TO
PAT and DON
PEG and PAT

INTRODUCTION

MINISTEPS TO MUSIC, Phase II, introduces three notes in the Treble Clef and four in the Bass Clef to complete a playing range of two octaves. The purpose of the sharp, flat and natural signs is explained by extended example. A descriptive essay in repetitive chromatic tone-colour, "Japanese Fan", summarises the function of accidentals and is a "nut-shell" illustration which pupils might profitably analyze.

Both hands are treated as of equal importance to provide the groundwork for eventual independence of the fingers. The pieces which include hand-crossing, must reveal no hesitant fumbling by the player. It is also important that the cross-over note struck, especially if it is a minim, should be sustained for its full time-value. On a rising phrase the tendency is to hasten the tempo, strike the cross-over note *marcato* and clip its musical value by a fraction or two.

If the author's system of CLOSE-PHASED GRADING has been taught in lesson sequence, such departure in interpreting the notation should not occur.

Upon completion of MINISTEPS TO MUSIC, Phase II, the student will have learned :—

1. How to name and play the additional notes which increase the reading range to two octaves.

2. To assess the time-value of the quaver.
3. To interpret the purpose of sharps, flats and naturals.
4. Key-colour changes effected in :—
    G Major — F Major
5. How to read and play two-note chords.
6. Keyboard freedom by crossing the left hand over the right.
7. The musical meaning of *Da capo al fine*.

W. M. Co., 8449

MARCH OF THE PALACE GUARDS
(Review)

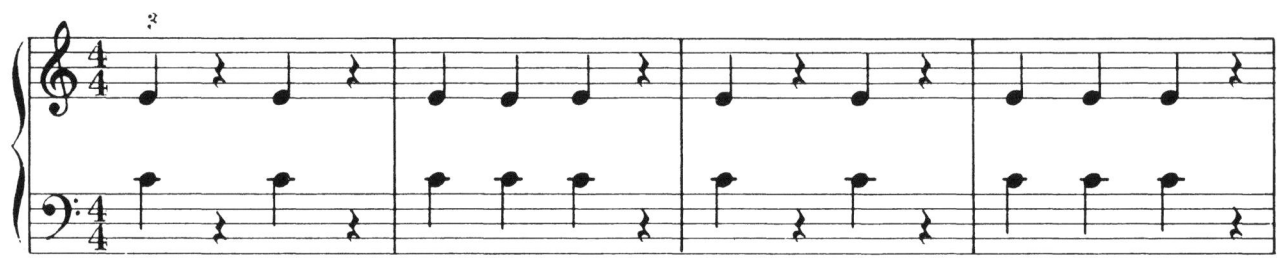

Try to give slightly more emphasis to the left hand in the middle eight bars.

A NEW C

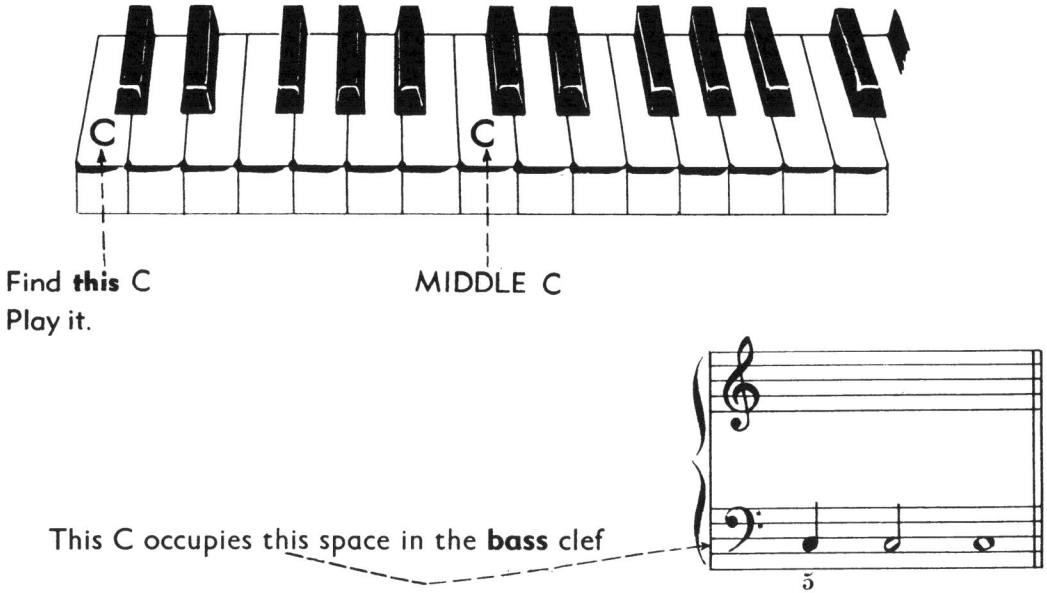

Find **this** C
Play it.

MIDDLE C

This C occupies this space in the **bass** clef

The **left** hand plays this note even though the stem is pointing up.

In the bass clef notes on the third line or below are written this way.
Play this C with the **finger marked 5 of your left** hand.

THE CLOCK

Tick, Tock, Tick, Tock, goes the clock.

Will it ev-er, ev-er, stop? Ding, Dong, Ding. Ding, Dong, Ding.

SUBMARINES

STILL ANOTHER C

MIDDLE C   Now play **this** C

Here are some pictures of this C.

This C is in this space in the **treble** clef

The **right** hand plays this note even though the stem is pointing down.

In the treble clef notes on the third line or above are written this way.

Play this C with the **finger marked 5** of your **right** hand.

W. M. Co., 8449

SLEEPY HEAD

TELEPHONE POLES

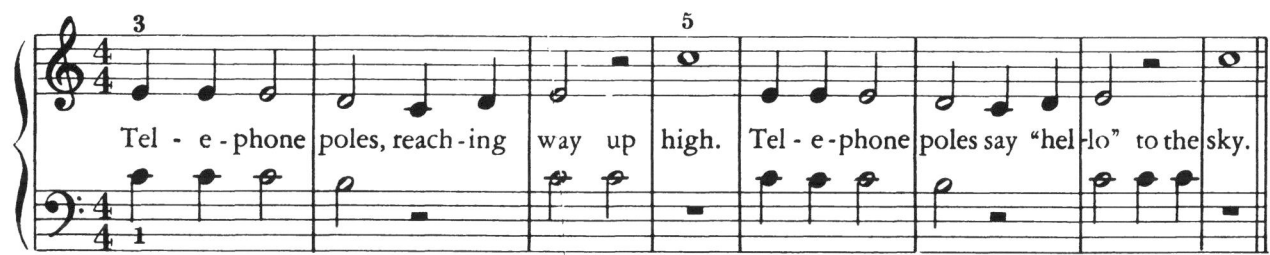

TWO BIG BLACKBIRDS

NOTE-READING REVIEW

Here are pictures of postal boxes which you might meet when on holiday abroad.

Read the notes on the front of each postbox.

Write the name of each note directly underneath.

If you get them all right, the postman will know where to deliver your letters.

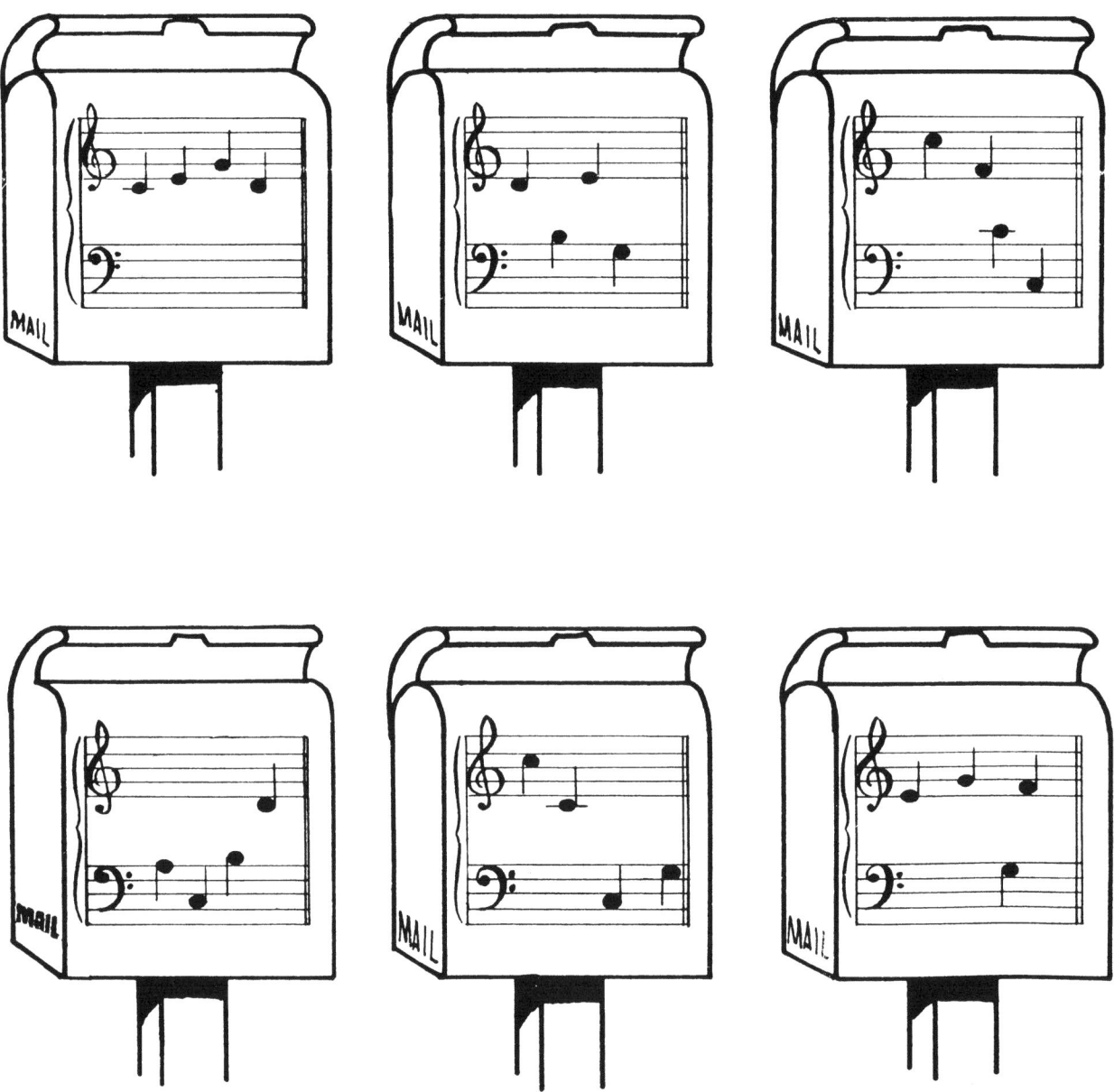

KITES

Look at these kites.

To fly well, they must be balanced just right.

To **play** well, we must know **note values** well.

Put as many bows on the tail of each kite as there are **counts** to the **notes** in each kite.

A note like this ♩ gets one count.

So that you will know how to begin, the first is finished for you

FROGS

Each frog croaks **four** bars.

They are croaking in either $\frac{2}{4}$ $\frac{3}{4}$ or $\frac{4}{4}$ time.

Write the correct **time signatures** before each line.

Write the **counts** under the **notes** and **rests**—like this

F ON KEYBOARD

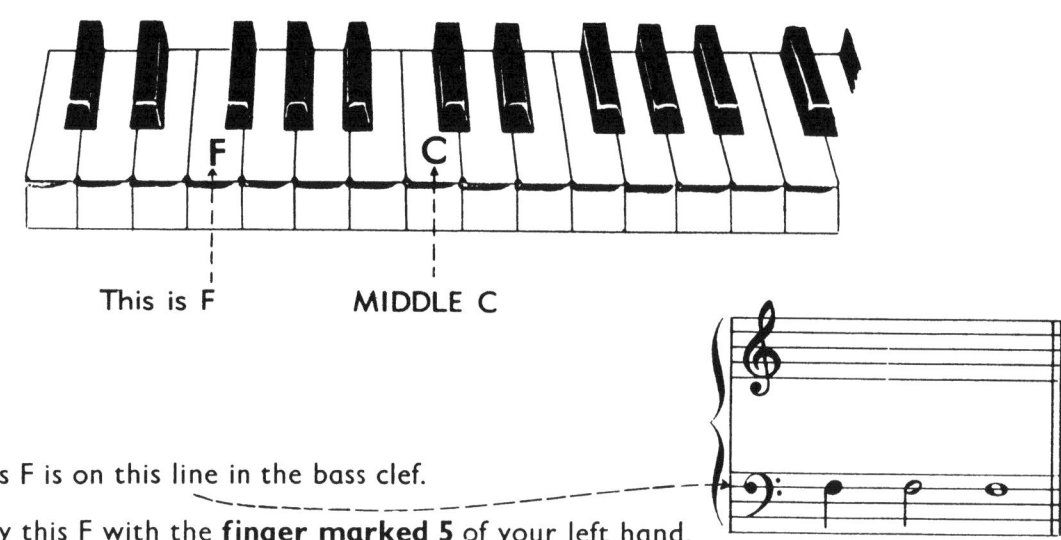

This is F MIDDLE C

This F is on this line in the bass clef.

Play this F with the **finger marked 5** of your left hand.

WHEN I TAKE A TRIP

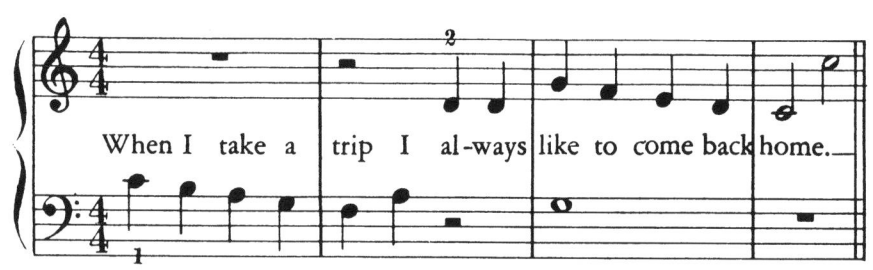

When I take a trip I al-ways like to come back home.

WALTZ

THE FLAT SIGN

This is a **flat** sign ♭

When a flat is placed **before** a note, play the **nearest** key to the **left of the note.**

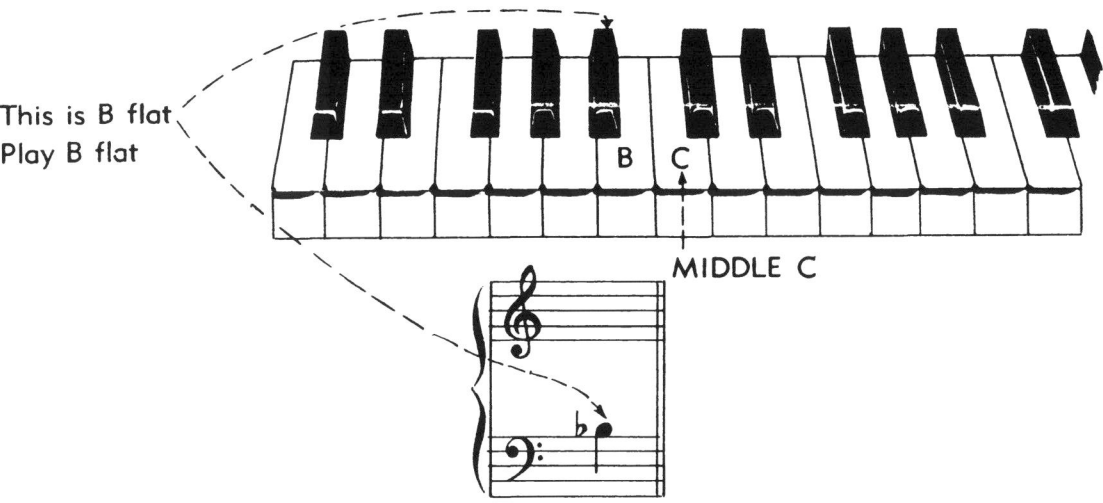

This is B flat
Play B flat

MIDDLE C

If this B flat is repeated in the same bar *without* the flat sign ♮, it must again be played as B flat.
After a bar-line the note must have another flat sign **before** it if it is to be played as B flat.

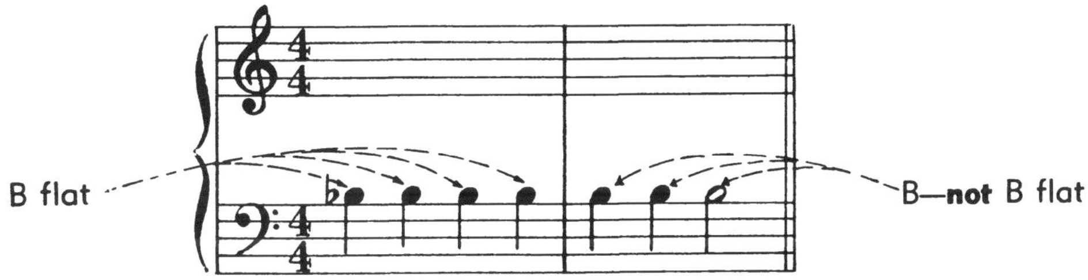

B flat .... B—**not** B flat

HALLOWEEN

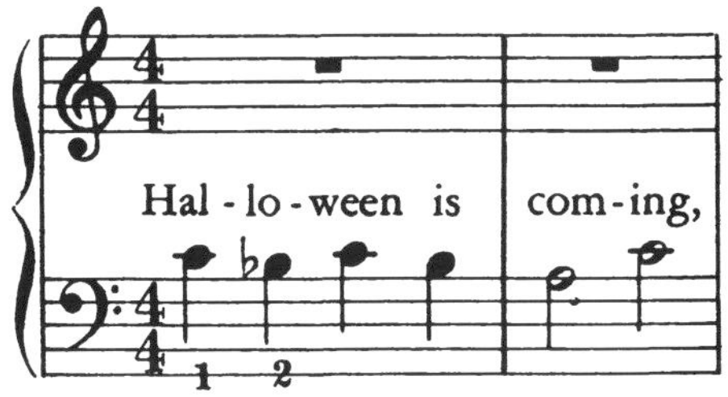

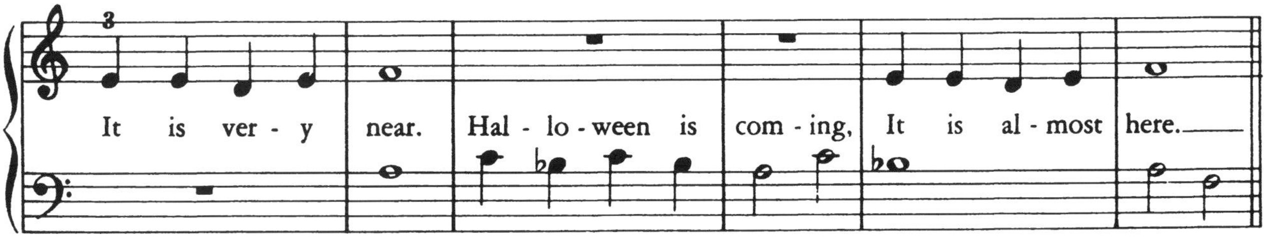

Hal-lo-ween is com-ing, It is ver-y near. Hal-lo-ween is com-ing, It is al-most here.

THE NATURAL SIGN

This is a natural sign ♮

When a **natural** sign is placed **before** a note that has been flattened it cancels the flat.

FUZZY LITTLE CATERPILLAR

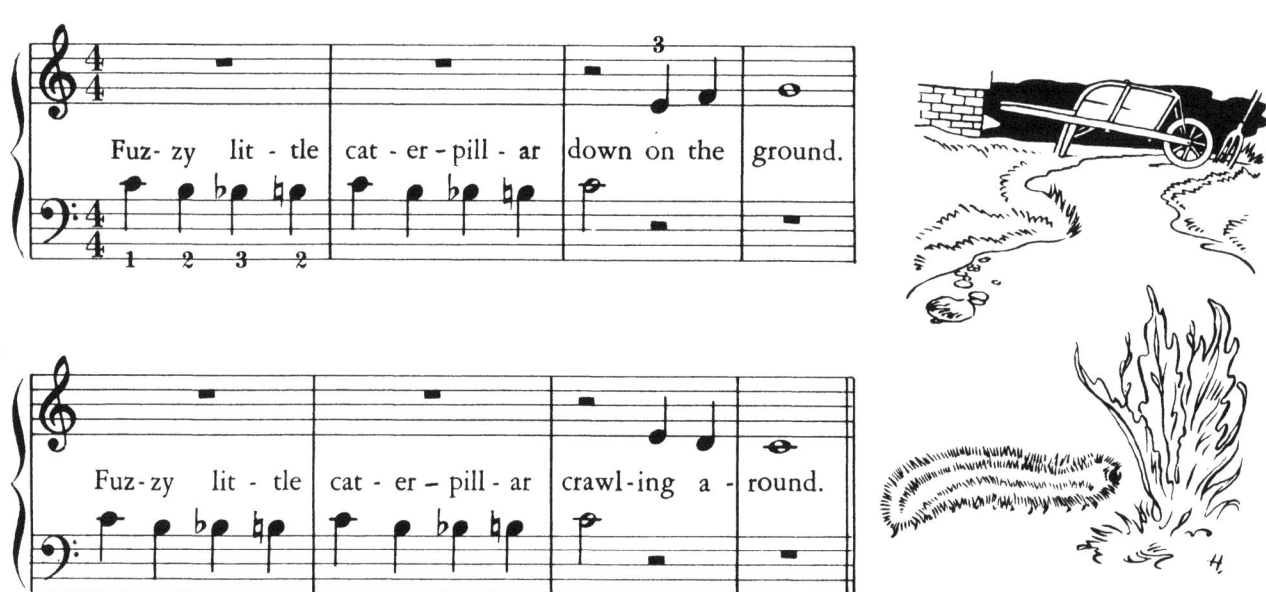

THE FLAT SIGN IN THE KEY SIGNATURE—F Major

When a flat sign is placed next to the **clef signs** (to the right), it becomes the **key signature.**

One flat is the **key of F major.** This flat note is B.

When you see one flat in the key **signature,** you must remember to flatten every B.

F Major Key Signature

JOLLY LITTLE PENGUINS

W. M. Co., 8449

MY VENETIAN BLINDS

My ven-e-tian blinds hide ev'-ry-thing from view,

I will pull the cord and let the sun-shine through.

EVERY BUSY LAWNMOWER

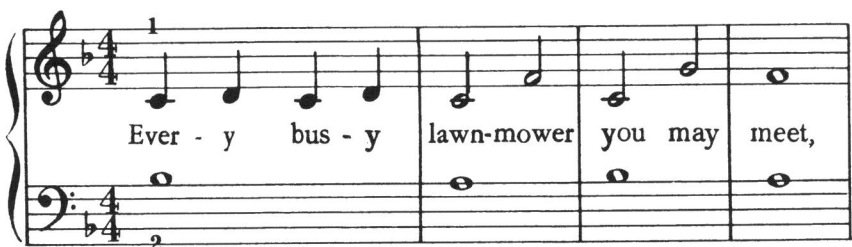

Ever-y bus-y lawn-mower you may meet,

Gives the grass a hair-cut, Keeps it ver-y neat.

QUAVERS

Here is a **quaver** (a **running** note) ♪ Notice the little hook or flag on the stem.

A quaver gets **one half a count.**

It takes **two** quavers to get **one** count.

Sometimes when there are two quavers together, instead of making them like this ♪ ♪ they are hooked together, and look like this ♫

When they are **joined** together like this ♫ the **two notes get one count** ♫

                                                                                                      One

Here is a piece that has quavers in $\frac{2}{4}$ time.

Count it—and **clap** as you count. Then **play** it and **count** it.

Play it s l o w l y so that you will be able to keep good time when you reach the quavers.

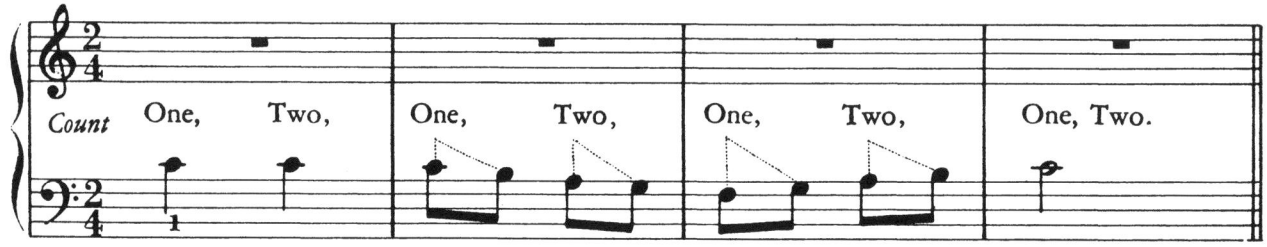

Quavers may also be joined together like this

Count them—and **clap** as you count. Then **play** and **count** them.

Here is some music in $\frac{4}{4}$ time for you to count and play.

Play it **s l o w l y**.

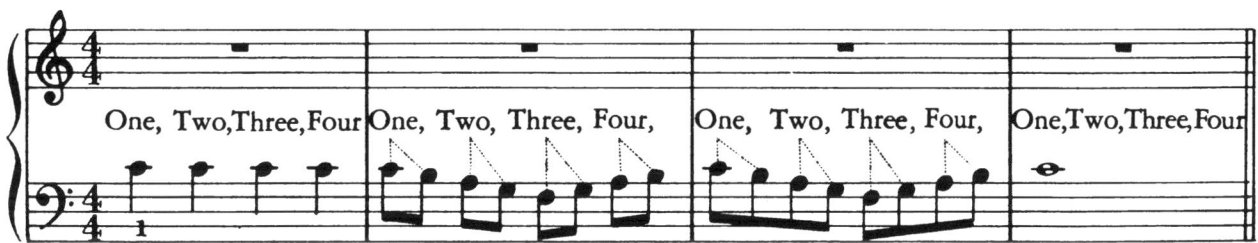

Here is music in $\frac{3}{4}$ time.

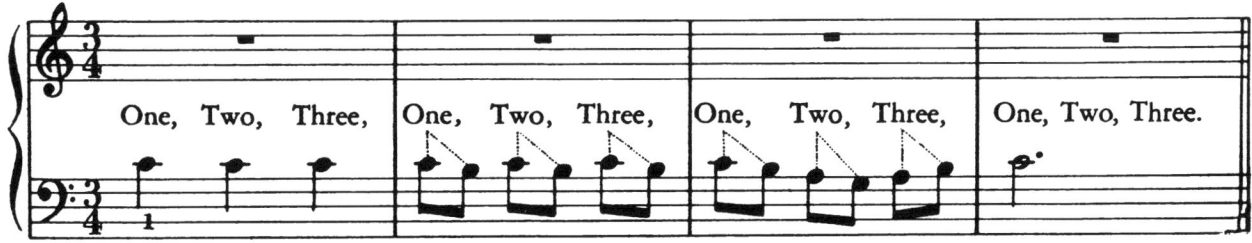

JOLLY LITTLE ROLLER COASTER

THE SHARP SIGN

This is a **sharp** sign ♯

When a sharp is placed **before a note,** play the **nearest** key to the **right of the note.**

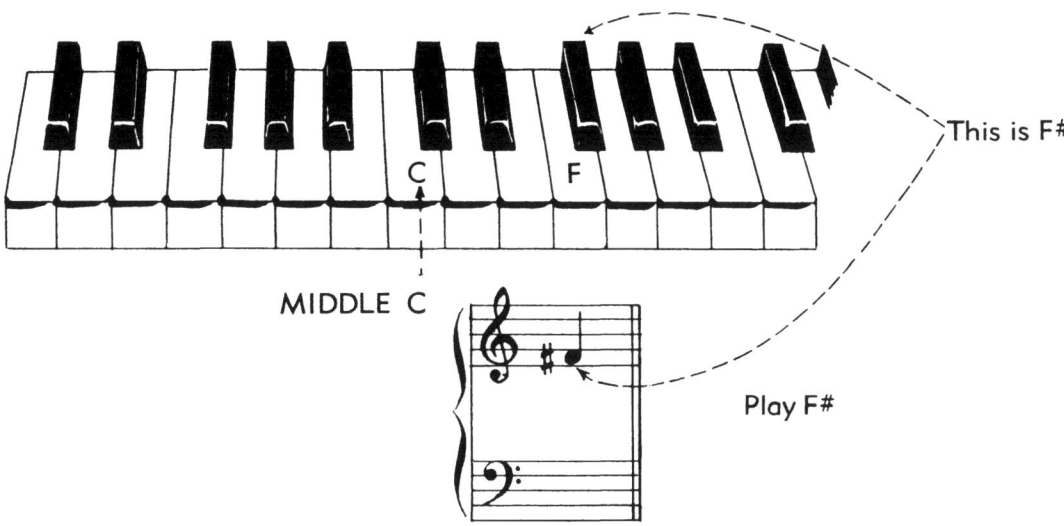

If this F sharp is repeated in the same bar **without** the sharp sign ♯, it must again be played as F sharp! **After** a bar-line the note must have **another** sharp sign **before** it if it is to be played as F sharp.

F sharp — ... — F—**not** F sharp

SLEEPY HEAD

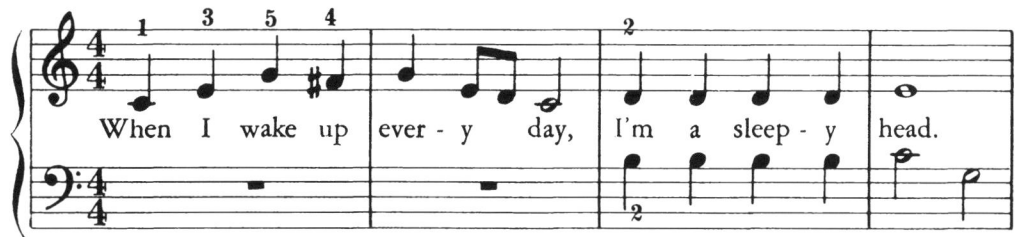

When I wake up ever-y day, I'm a sleep-y head.

When I wake up ever-y day, I want to stay in bed.

W. M. Co., 8449

AUTUMN LEAVES

Aut-umn leaves are fall-ing fall-ing, fall-ing.

Aut-umn leaves are fall-ing, on the ground.

When a natural sign ♮ is placed **before** a note that has been sharpened it **cancels** the sharp.

BABIES

Bab-ies can't do ver-y much. They can't ev-en walk!

Bab-ies can't do ver-y much, They can't ev-en talk!

W. M. Co., 8449

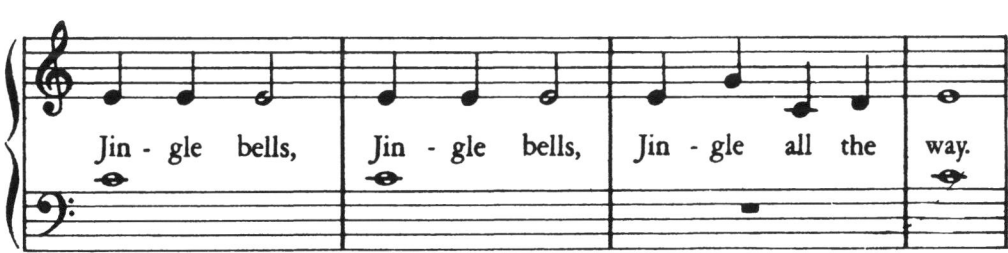

THE SHARP SIGN IN THE KEY SIGNATURE—G Major

When a sharp sign is placed next to the **clef signs**, (to the right), it becomes the **key signature**.

One sharp is the key of G major. This sharp note is F.

When you see one sharp in the **key signature**, you must remember to **sharpen every F**.

LITTLE SQUIRREL

Little squir-rel in the sun, You're nim-ble as can be.
Eat-ing nuts from ever-y one, Come, come and vi-sit me.

ICE SKATING

THREE BLIND MICE

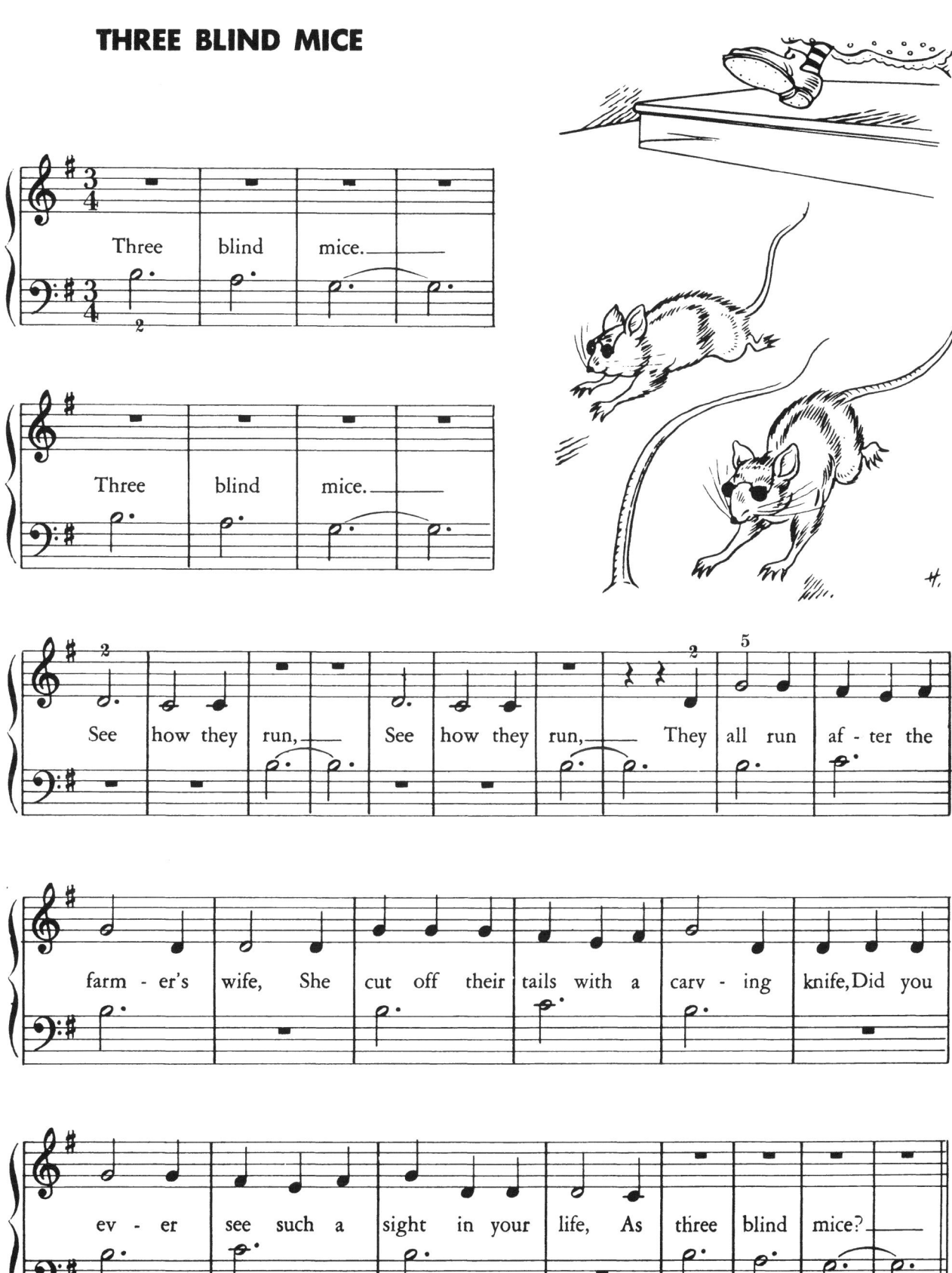

ELEPHANTS

Here are some elephants.

How many logs can each one carry?

This is the way to find out.

Each one can carry as many logs as there are **counts** in the **notes** on his blanket.

A note like this ♩ gets one count.

Write how many logs each one can carry in the space under each elephant.

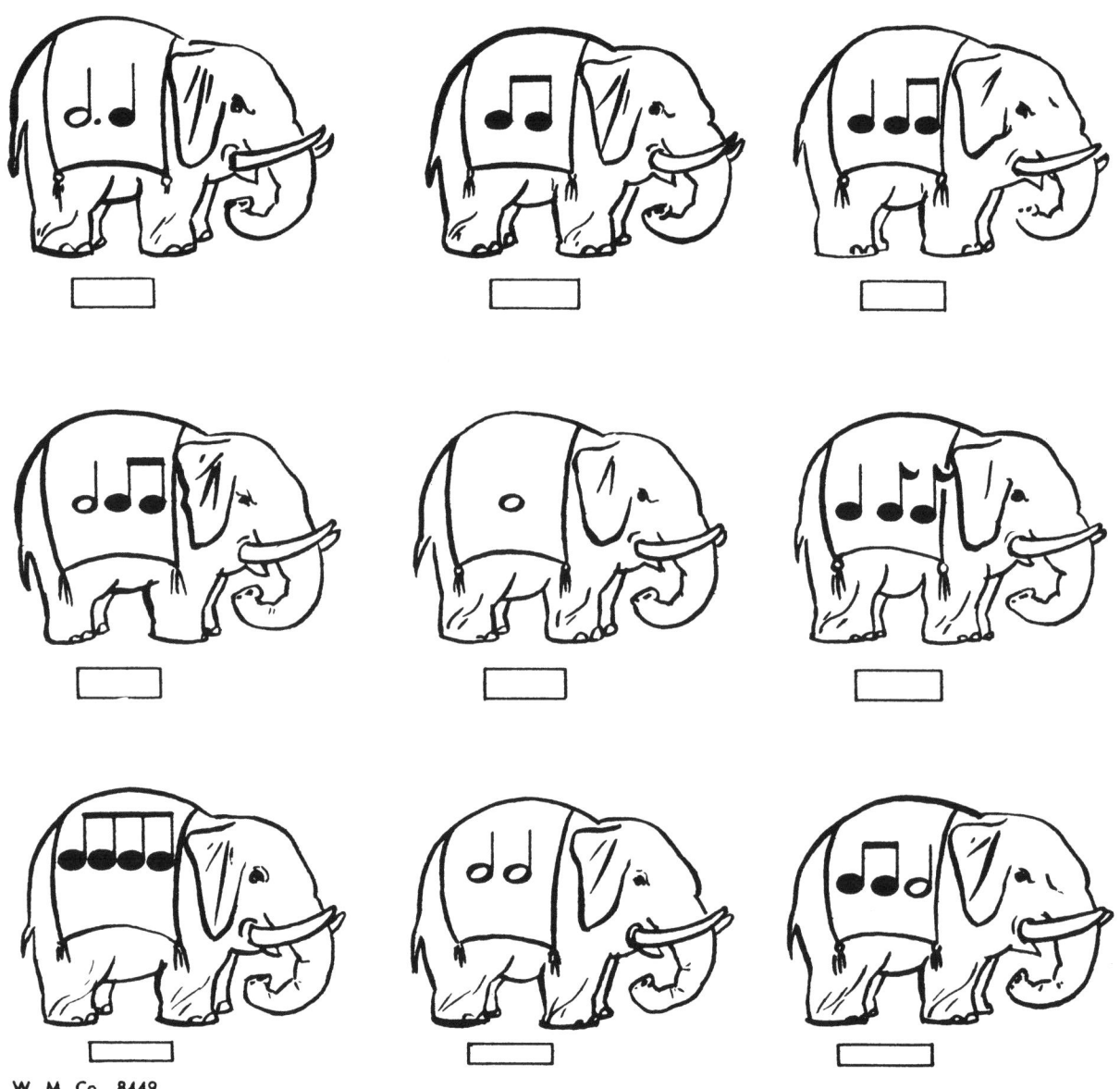

HENS

Here are some hens.

Each hen clucks four bars.

They cluck in either $\frac{2}{4}$ $\frac{3}{4}$ or $\frac{4}{4}$ time.

Write the correct time signature before each line.

Then write the counts under the notes—like this:

W. M. Co., 8449

TWO-NOTE CHORDS

When **two** or **more notes** are played **together,** they are called a **chord.**

Here is a two note chord

Here are some pieces with two note chords.

TUNE OF THE TUBA

I GO TO SCHOOL

I go to school ev-ery morn - ing, with my friend.

FLAT – SHARP – AND NATURAL SIGNS

REMEMBER:—

When a flat sign ♭ is placed before a note, play the **nearest** key to the **left** of the note.

When a sharp sign ♯ is placed before a note, play the **nearest** key to the **right** of the note.

When a natural sign ♮ is placed before a note, it **cancels** the effect of a sharp or flat sign.

FOLDING FAN

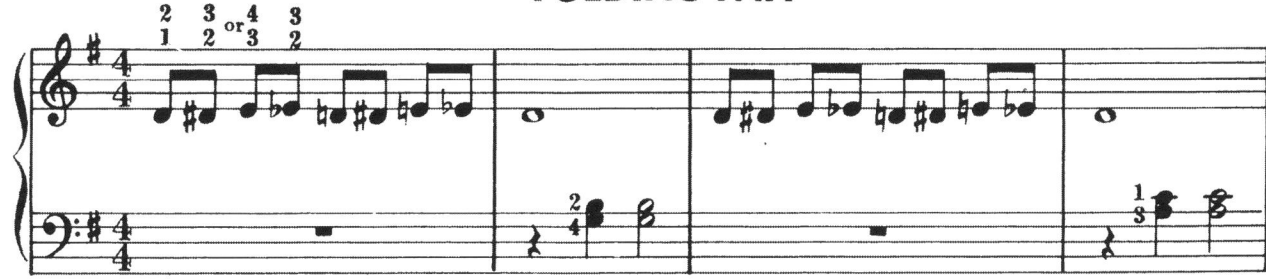

A NEW E

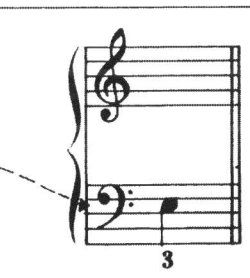

This new note E is in this space of the bass clef.

Play this C with the **fifth** finger of your left hand.

Again play this C and then the E above it.

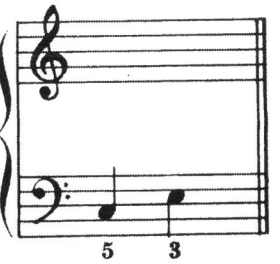

Play this E with your **third** finger.

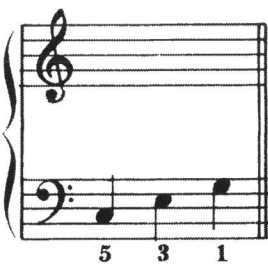

Now play these three notes.

W. M. Co., 8449

IN THE GYMNASIUM

COLOURED LIGHTS

SKIP, SKIP, AND AWAY WE GO

W.-M. Co., 8449

A NEW D

Play C above with the **fifth finger** of your **left** hand.

Now play the **next white note above** it.

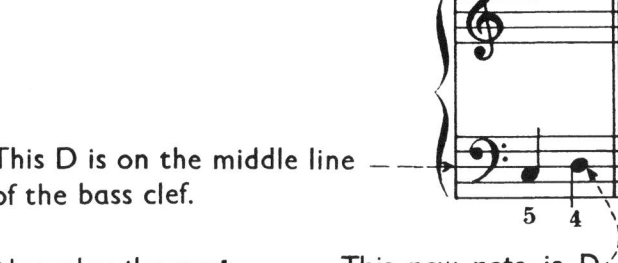

This D is on the middle line of the bass clef.

This new note is D. Play it with the **fourth** finger of your left hand.

SONG OF THE CELLO

RAINBOW

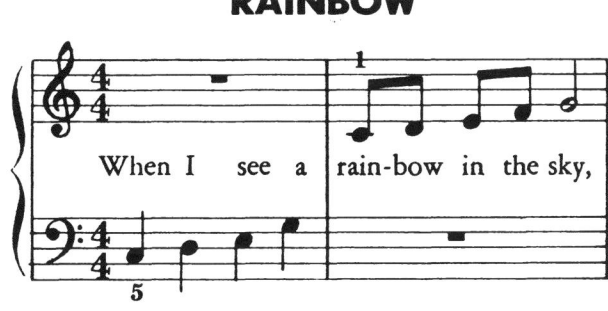

When I see a rain-bow in the sky,

Beau-ti-ful and bright. When I see a rain-bow in the sky, It's a pret-ty sight.

W. M. Co., 8449

EARLY IN THE MORNING

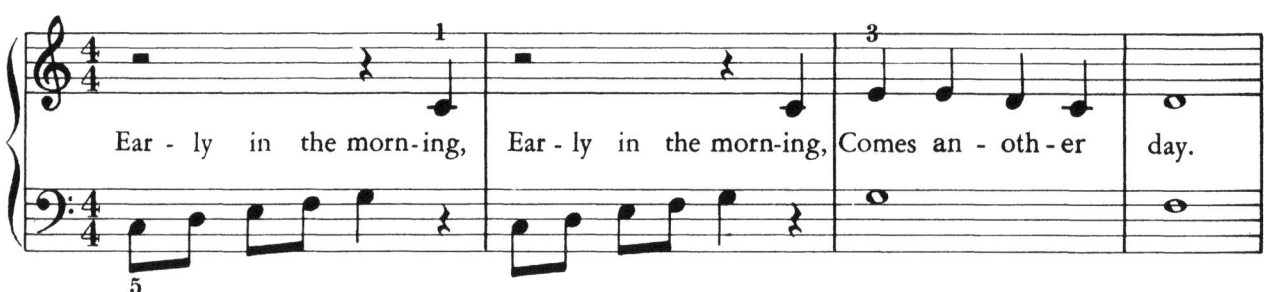
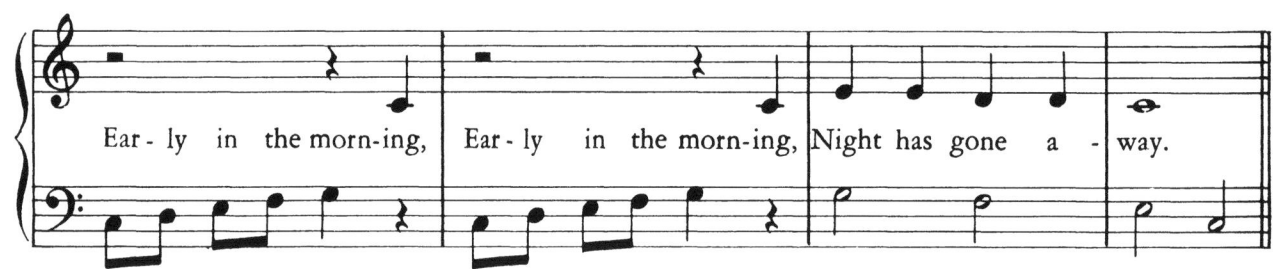

ARE YOU SLEEPING

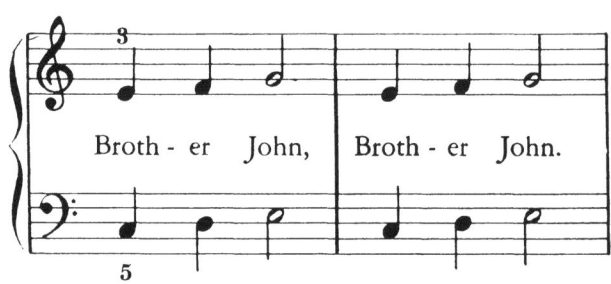

NEW NOTE (in the treble clef)

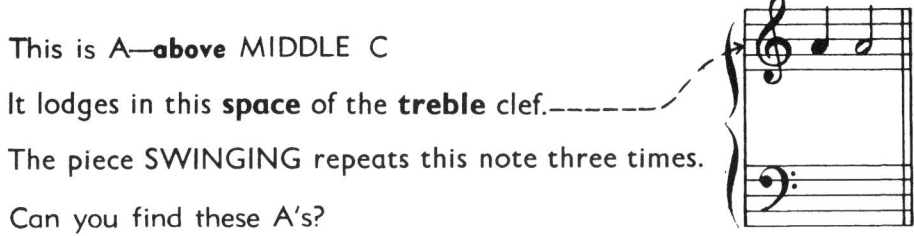

This is A—**above** MIDDLE C

It lodges in this **space** of the **treble** clef.

The piece SWINGING repeats this note three times.

Can you find these A's?

Notice that the letters (l.h.) are in certain places in this piece.

These letters (l.h.) mean that your **left** hand must play this note.

To do this, your **left hand must cross over your right hand.**

The dotted lines in the first two bars are a guide to help you cross your **left** hand **over** your **right** to play the new note A.

SWINGING

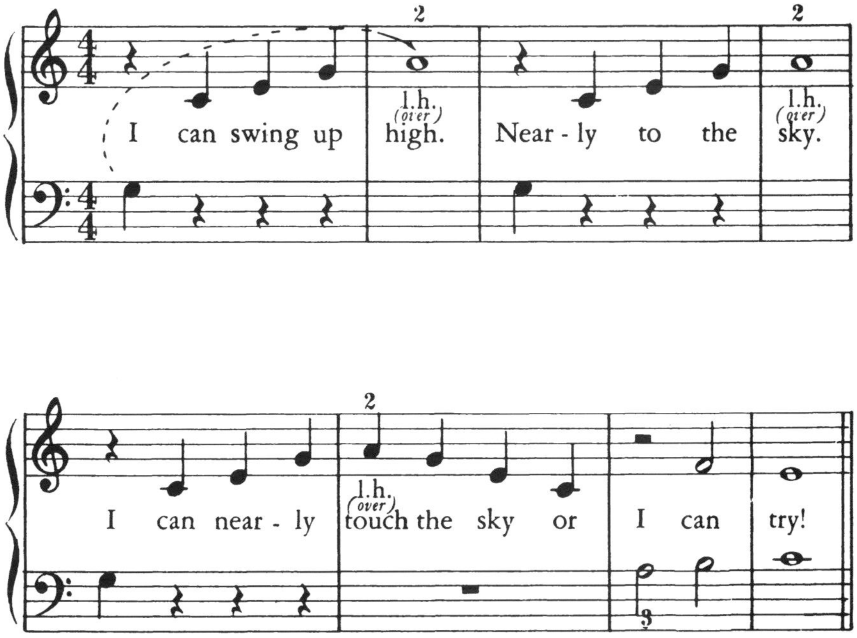

I can swing up high. Near-ly to the sky.

I can near-ly touch the sky or I can try!

CHANGE OF FINGERING

Finger markings are a **great** help to you when you play the piano.

Always use the fingers that are **marked** for you when you play.

Your playing will sound **smooth,** and it will be **easier** for you.

Notice that you begin playing the next piece by using the finger marked 3 on F.

If you **begin** this way, you will be able to play A with your **right** hand, using the finger marked 5.

EVERY SUNDAY MORNING

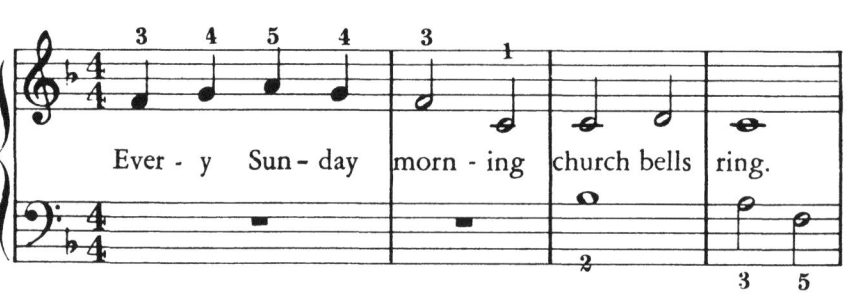

Did you remember to look at the **key signature?**

In which key are you playing?

Which note had to be flattened? Did you do it as you played?

D. C. al Fine

Look at the last bar of this piece.

Notice what is printed under it—**D.C. al fine.** This is Italian and in full it reads—*Da Capo al fine.*

When you see this in a piece, it means that you must go back to the beginning of the piece again —and play it until you come to the word **"fine"**.

You will find the word "Fine" in the eighth bar of this piece.

"Fine"—pronounced *fee-neh*—means that the piece ends there.

FUNNY LITTLE RABBIT

Did you remember to **cross** your **left** hand in the last bar of the **third** and **fourth** lines?

ROCKING CHAIR

When I rock in my old rock-ing chair.

I pre-tend I can go an-y-where.

Fine

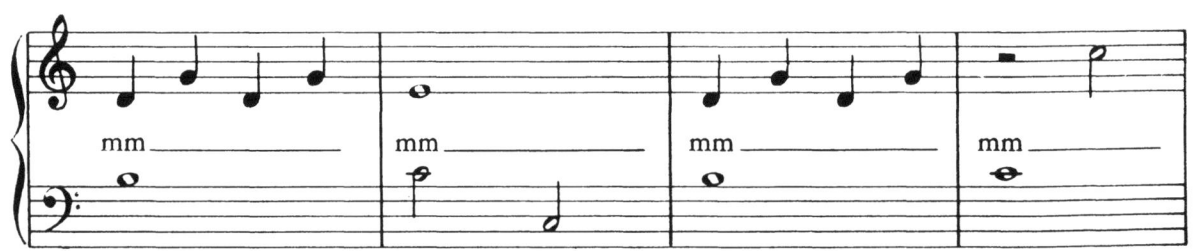

mm — mm — mm — mm

mm — mm — mm — mm

D.C. al fine

CHRISTMAS STOCKINGS

Here are some Christmas Stockings.

How many presents will there be in each stocking on Christmas morning?

This is how to find out.

There will be as many presents as there are **counts** in the **notes** on each stocking.

Write the number of counts on the top of each stocking.

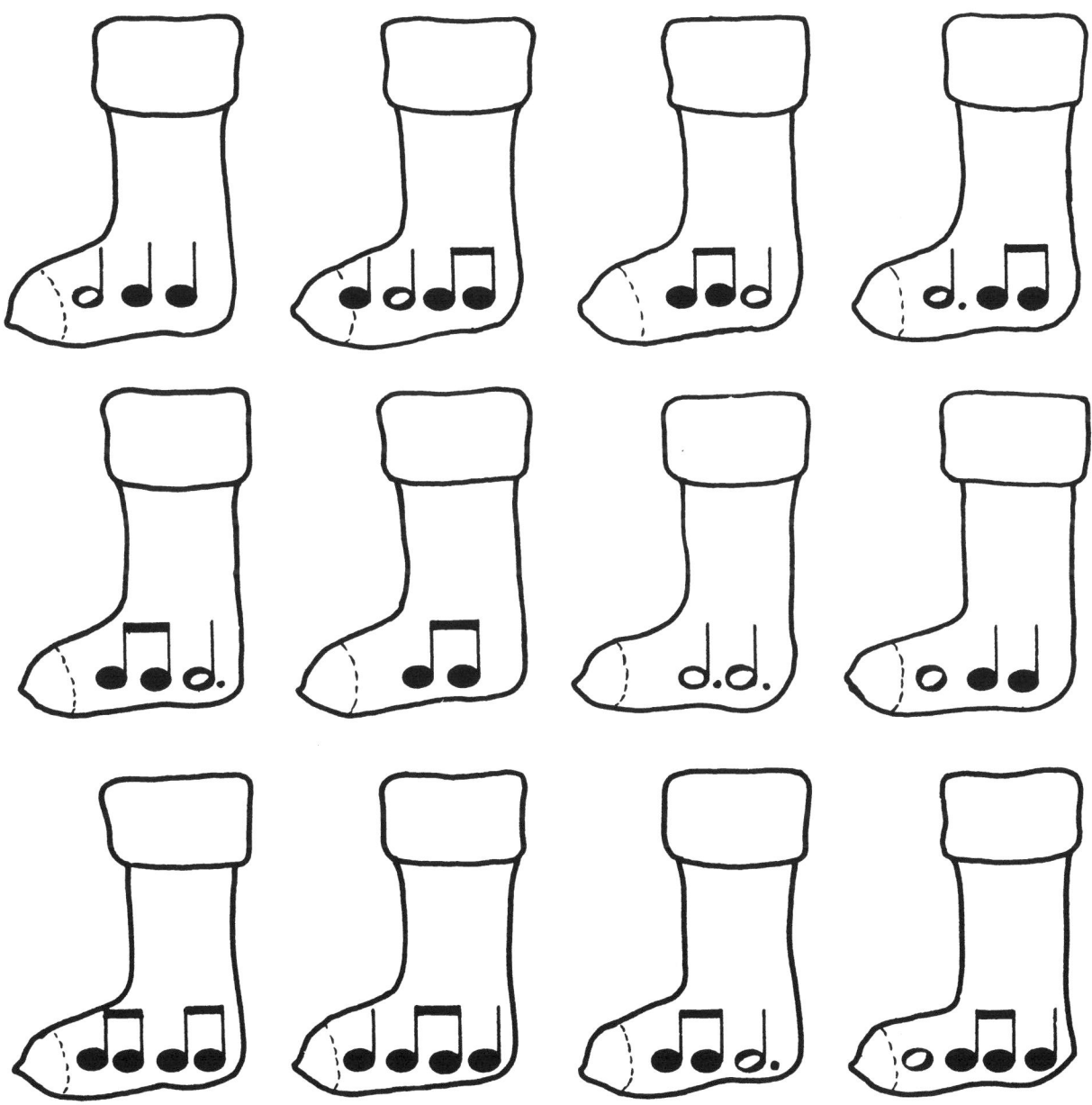

BIRDS

Each of these birds sings four bars.

They sing in either $\frac{2}{4}$ $\frac{3}{4}$ or $\frac{4}{4}$ time.

Write the correct time signature before each line.

Then write the counts under each note.

A BALLOON

Write the name of each note under that note
If you get one wrong, it means the balloon pops!

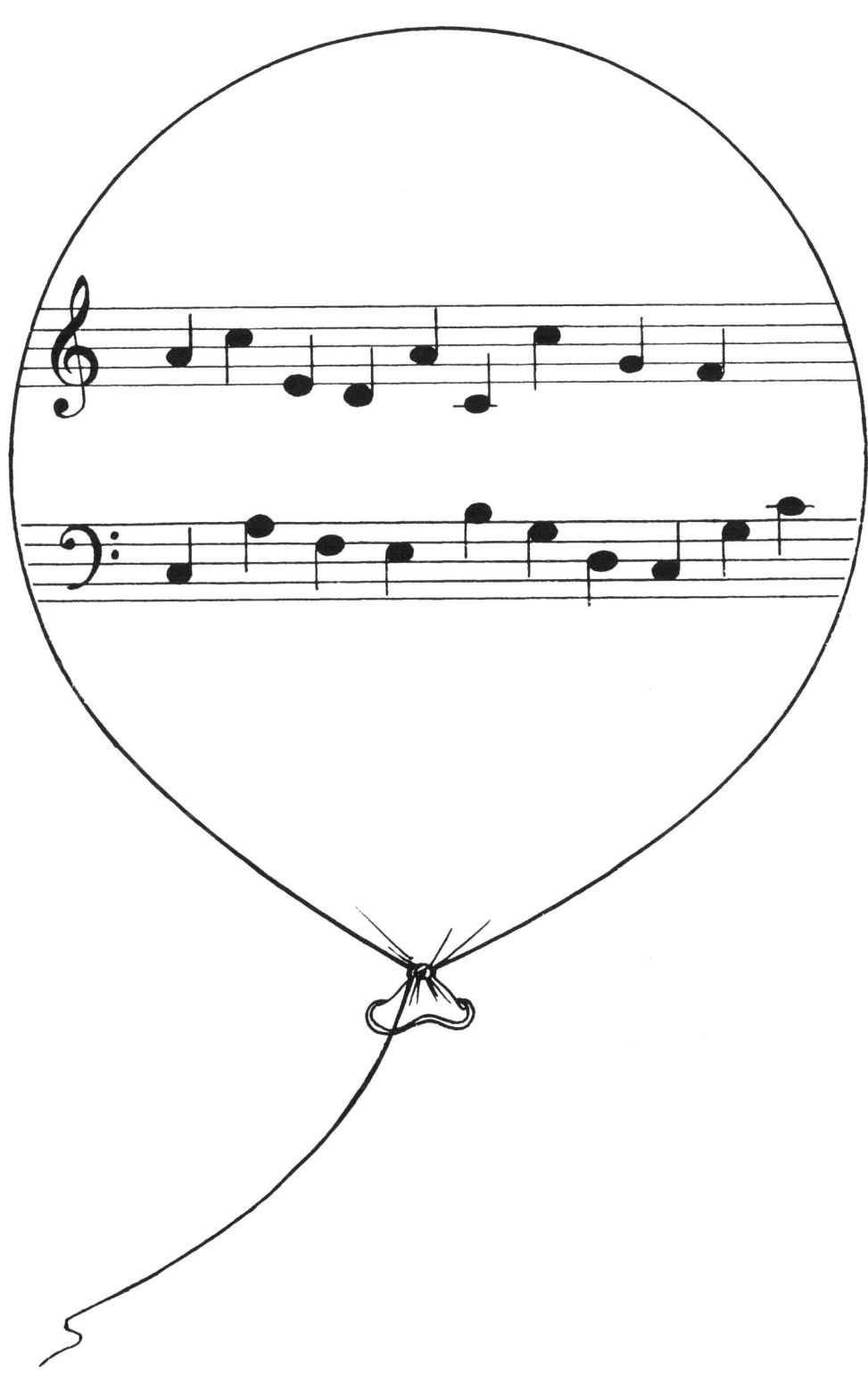

PUMPKIN FACES

Write the names of the notes below each Pumpkin Face.

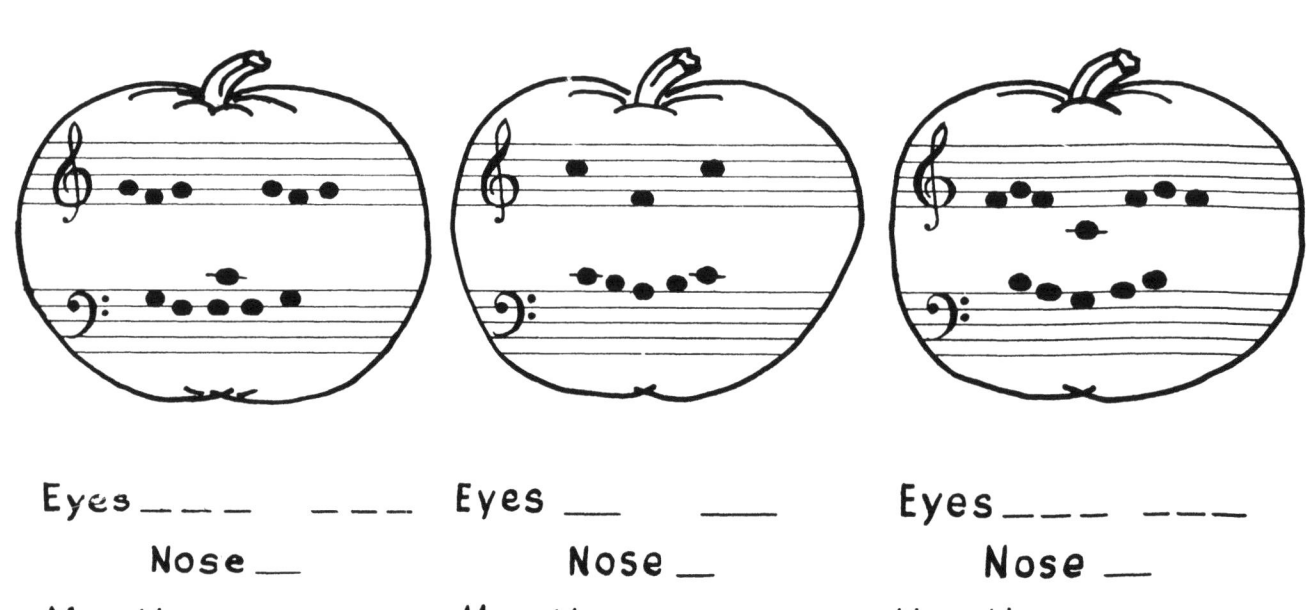

Eyes ___ ___   Eyes ___ ___   Eyes ___ ___
　Nose ___　　　　　Nose ___　　　　　Nose ___
Mouth ___ ___ ___ ___   Mouth ___ ___ ___ ___ ___   Mouth ___ ___ ___ ___ ___

Eyes ___ ___   ___ ___   Eyes ___   ___   Eyes ___ ___   ___ ___
　Nose ___　　　　　Nose ___　　　　　Nose ___
Mouth ___ ___ ___ ___ ___   Mouth ___ ___ ___ ___ ___   Mouth ___ ___ ___ ___ ___

A NEW B (in the treble clef)

This is B **above** MIDDLE C

It lodges on this line of the treble clef

When you play the pieces below,

make sure you use the correct fingers.

LITTLE MOUSE

Nib-ble, Nib-ble, Nib-ble, Goes a lit-tle mouse.

Nib-ble, Nib-ble, Nib-ble, All a-round the house.

CLOWNS

W. M. Co., 8449

PRAIRIE SONG

When I ride on the plains far a-way, I sing a far a-way song.
When I ride on the plains far a-way, I sing it all the day long.
Fine

List-en to the song of the prair-ie, List-en to a song far a-way.
List-en to the song of the prair-ie, Hear the song to-day.
D.C. al fine

MINISTEPS TO MUSIC—Phase 2, Review

Your teacher will give you this final check-up.

Which notes require the following counts:—

    1 count
    2 counts
    3 counts
    4 counts
    ½ a count

Write **two** notes that get **one** count.

Which rests require the following counts?

    1 count
    2 counts
    4 counts
    3 counts

Point to a :—

    sharp
    flat
    natural
    two note chord

Distinguish between the following key signatures :—

    F major
    C major
    G major

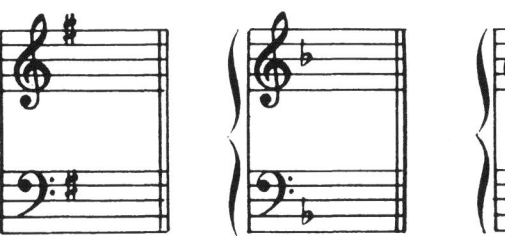

Explain what "D.C. al fine" means.

Explain what "l.h." means.

W. M. Co., 8449